1

Alicia was about to give birth to twins. She was only 15 years old and time was

fading away. "we have to do something." said the nurse. "what can we do?" asked the

doctor. "she will die if we don't do something." said the nurse.

Alicia gave out a scream. "it's time or she will die." said the nurse. "alright." said

the doctor. Within 30 minutes the twins were out. Alicia started to shake. "OH NO

SHE IS DYING!" said the nurse. But it was too late she was gone. "what are we going to

do?" asked the nurse. "give the babies to foster care." said the doctor. "No, I will take

them in" said the nurse. "fine just for a little while." said the doctor.

The Nurse took the twins home. Her husband was in his office when she came into

the office. "what do you got there?" asked her husband. "I found our children." she said.

"what?" asked her husband. "they are twins." said the nurse. "how are you going to pay to

have twins?" asked her husband. "their mother just died." said the nurse. "now Jessie I told you. You can't bring every child that needs a home." said her husband. "David

Nobody will want them because they have down's syndrome. Their mother died during

child birth. She was only 15 years old." said Jessie. "and how are you going to take care

of two kids with down's syndrome?" asked David. "I will check into some places that

have a school for kids that are disabled." said Jessie.

Just then one of the babies started to shake. "OH MY GOSH!" said Jessie running

to the baby. "what is wrong with him?" asked David. "he has seizures." said Jessie. "what

are we going to do? This is a bad idea Jessie." said David. "no, it's not David. I can't have

any kids so I am adopting them." said Jessie.

A few weeks went by. And the paper work is going well. Jessie named the baby

girl Grace and the boy Jay-Jay. As they started to grow weeks turn into months. Then it

was their first birthday. The adoption date was almost there.

One day there was a phone call. The father of Grace and Jay-Jay wanted the kids

back. Jessie started to cry. David came into the house. "Jessie what is wrong?" asked

David. "he wants them." said Jessie. "Then fight for them. They are our children." said

David. Jessie went to court and saw the father of Jay-Jay and Grace. He looked older like

in his 50's "hello you must be Jessica. "said the man. "yes" said Jessie. "how did my

daughter die?" said the man "she died of a seizure." said Jessie. "she didn't have them."

said the man. "are you the father of the twins?" asked Jessie. "yes" said the man. "did you know she was 15 years old." said Jessie. "yes." said the man. "do you know you can be

put in prison for rape?" asked Jessie. "no, I just want my children back." said the man.

"they are my children now." said Jessie. "what do you mean they are your children?"

asked the man. "you left your daughter at a hospital in the middle of nowhere. And now

she's dead you want her children back after a year went by. No, I am sorry you can't get

them back I will not give my children back to a no-good man like you." said Jessie. "we

will see about that." said the man. They went into the court room. Jessie told the judge

that the babies need special care and that the "father" of her children don't know how to

take care of them. "the judge agreed with Jessie that the twins would be better off being

with her. "YOU WILL PAY FOR THIS." said the twin's father. "why do you say that?"

asked Jessie. "because I will always get my way." said the man. "we will see about that."

said Jessie. "you know you will lose." said the man. "if you ever come near my family I

will put you in jail." said Jessie. "oh, I am scared." said the guy.

Just then a cop walked by. "what is going to here?" asked the cop. "she has my kids." said

the man. "he raped his daughter and left her for dead." said Jessie "do you have proof that

this did happen." said the cop. "I know his daughter Alicia died giving birth to his

children." said Jessie. "and how old was she?" asked the cop. "15 years old that is why

both Grace and Jay-Jay have down's syndrome and they have special needs that he can't

give them." said Jessie. "do you have proof that she was raped." said the cop. "right here."

said Jessie she gave him the file about Alicia. "Well sir I am going to have to take you in."

"what do you mean I didn't do anything to that kid." said the guy. "what is your name

sir?" asked the cop." "my name doesn't matter. I want my kids back." said the man "they

are not your kids anymore. I am Grace and Jay-Jay mother now." said Jessie. "that's

enough think about the babies they have no mother and all you people do is fight." said the cop. "sorry sir." said Jessie. "now tell me your name." said the cop. "my name is Jonathan

White. But people call me Jon." said the man. "I know you. You're the guy with all the

kids." said the cop. "that's right." said Jon Proudly. "you killed your own daughter by

raping her. Then left her for dead." said Jessie. "no, I didn't I never touched her." said Jon.

"give me A DNA test and tell me that you are not the father of Grace and Jay-Jay." said Jessie.

"who would name their kid those names?" asked Jon. "I would." said Jessie. "sir your

daughter had your children and if this is true you will be put into prison." said the cop.

"Alicia was never hurt by me or my wife." said Jon. "then why does the twins have

Down's syndrome?" asked Jessie "I have no clue why who care would even?" asked Jon. "I

care that's who." said Jessie. "are you their father?" asked the cop. "No." said Jon. "then

why did you say you were?" asked Jessie. "I mean I am their grandfather." said Jon. "no

you are their father Alicia told me before she had them, she said she was raped by her

father." said Jessie. "she is a liar." said Jon. "no she's not" said another girl. "who are you?" asked the cop. "I am her sister all the things he says are lies he got half his

daughters pregnant including me and Alicia." said the girl. "YOU ARE A LIAR!"

screamed Jon. "well sir you have to come with me" said the cop putting handcuffs on Jon.

"YOU WILL PAY FOR THIS!" screamed Jon. "how is my sister." said the girl. "I am

sorry honey but she died during childbirth." said Jessie. "Oh no did the baby make it."

asked the girl. "yes, she had twins, but they have down's syndrome." said Jessie. "what are

their names?" asked the girl. "Grace and Jay-Jay." said Jessie. "cute names." said the girl.

"what is your name?" asked Jessie. "Laura." said the girl. "did you say your dad raped you

too?' asked Jessie. "Yes." said Laura. "where is your mother." said Jessie. "she died when

we were young." said Laura. "why would he do something like this?" asked Jessie. "he

raped his sister and she gave birth to twins. But they died at birth, so I heard." said Laura

"he needs to be put behind bars." said Jessie.

2

Jessie took the twins home. "how did it go at the court house?" said David "it

went alright." said Jessie. "what's wrong?" asked David. "he is trying to take the twins

Away." said Jessie. "who?" asked David. "Alicia's father. The father of the twins." said

Jessie. "what for?" asked David. "because he is their father." said Jessie. "well can he take

them away?" asked David. "he could but I don't think it will happen." said Jessie.

Just then Jay-Jay started to have a seizer. She held him until it was done. "is he

alright?" asked David. "yes, I think so." said Jessie. Grace started to cry. There was a

knock on the door. Jessie got the door. "hello Jessica." said the man. "and you are." said

Jessie. "I have come for you." said the man. "what do you mean you have come to me?"

asked Jessie. Just then he opened his mouth he had fangs. She woke up to Grace crying.

"you alright Jessie?" asked David. "yeah I am fine." said Jessie.

Later that night Jessie had another dream. "Jessica…. Jessica. Where… are…. you.

I…. have….been….waiting…for….you." said the voice. "where are you." said Jessie.

"over…. here." said the voice. And a man showed up. "what do you want from me?"

asked Jessie. "you are the chosen one." said the man. "what do you mean. "I mean they

have chosen you to kill vampires." said the man "what? No way I am a mother of two

sick kids." said Jessie "your family must never know about this. Here is what you kill them

with don't tell anybody about this or the vampires will come after you." said the man and

he went away. When she woke up, she had a stake in her hand. She went to the closet and

hid the stake. David came into the room. "what are you doing?" asked David "DON'T

SEEK UP ON ME LIKE THAT." said Jessie. "what are you doing?" asked David. "I was

putting something away." said Jessie. "what is it?" asked David. "I can't say." said Jessie.

Going back to bed. "why not?" asked David. "Because this person I know gave it to me

and he don't want anybody to see it." said Jessie "why can't you show me?" asked David

"because this person said not to." said Jessie and she turned off the light.

All though the night Jessie was having nightmares.

"Jessica…. Jessica where are you." said the voice. Jessie looked over at her husband.

When she looked over at, he was watching her. "why are you staring at me?" asked

Jessie. "I have been waiting for the moment." said David. "what?" asked Jessie. "I know

your secret." said David "what do you mean?" asked Jessie. "I know you are the chosen

one you are the one that kills vampires." said David. "how did you know?" asked Jessie.

"because I am a vampire." said David. He showed his fangs and she woke up. When she

looked at David he was still sleeping. She let out a deep breath.

The next morning Jessica was getting the kids to go to their school when David

came down. "you're up early." said David. "couldn't sleep." said Jessie. "another

nightmare." said David. Jessica looked at her husband weird. "I never told you I was

having nightmares." said Jessica. "you did last night." said David "no I didn't David."

said Jessica. "ok, ok fine by me." said David sitting in his chair waiting for breakfast.

While David was at work and Jay-Jay and Grace was at school Jessica took a nap.

"Jessica…. Jessica where are you I need you." said the voice. "where are you?" asked

Jessica. "I am right here." said the voice and a man dressed in a suit and Cape. "what do

you want from me?" asked Jessica "I want you to be my Dark Angel." said the man. "why

I am a mother not a vampire killer." said Jessica. "you are the chosen one." said the man.

"but I have a family to take care of." said Jessica "there is nothing you can do about this."

said the man. "LIKE HELL THERE'S NOT!" yelled Jessica. "you can't tell anyone." said

the man. "why?" asked Jessica "Because you will be dead yourself." said the man. "will I

get help?" asked Jessica. "there are 2 other woman that are the chosen one they will come

to you in a few days." said the man. "what about the dream that I had last night is David a

vampire?" asked Jessica. "no, he's not they are trying to get you to kill him." said the man.

"but why my husband?" said Jessica. "because they want you to be weak." said the man.

"how can I control the dreams?" asked Jessica. "you can't control them all." said the man.

"will he die if I don't stop them?" asked Jessica. "No." said the man. And he was gone.

"WAIT PLEASE DON'T GO!" said Jessica

when she woke up Matt was standing over her looking at her. "David what are you

doing?" asked Jessica. "you tell me." said David. "you forgot to pick up the kids." said

David. "oh, I am sorry I guess I was tired." said Jessica "I guess so when you forget to pick up your kids." said David. "I am sorry." said Jessica. "the way you have been acting

lately I am not surprised that you didn't." said David. Jessica started to cry. "Hey what is

it why is you crying?" asked David. "Because I can't tell you or I will die." said Jessica.

"die?" asked David. "that is what the guy in my dream said." said Jessica.

3

A few weeks later there was a knock on the door.

"May I help you?" asked Jessica "are you Jessica?" asked the lady. "yes." said Jessica

"well my name is Lorie, and this is Karen." said Lorie. "come on in." said Jessica. "I know

you don't want to do this like any of us do." said Lorie. "yes, that is true." said Jessica.

"but we are the chosen ones." said Lorie. "so, what" said Jessica "if we don't kill the

vampires are lives with be vanished and we will become vampires ourselves." said Lorie.

"they want my boyfriend to be the bad guy." said Karen. "mine too." Said Lorie. "do you

have dreams about them becoming a Vampire?" asked Jessica "you have the same dream?" asked Lorie. "yes, and it scares me because I am scared that he is one." said

Jessica. "how do you know?" asked Lorie. "He said something about me having

nightmares when I didn't say nothing to him about it." said Jessica. "maybe he heard you

in your sleep?" asked Karen. "I don't like this. This is too much for me." said Jessica.

"there's nothing that can be done." said Lorie. "what about my kids?" asked Jessica

"where are they?" asked Lorie. "they are a special school for the handicapped they both

have down syndrome. Said Jessica. "Oh, how sad." said Lorie. "you don't look like a

person that would have any trouble with kids." said Karen. "they are adopted their mom

died when they were born." said Jessica "oh how sad." said Karen. "it's alright." said

Jessica. "Now why are we the chosen one?" asked Lorie. "I am not sure." said Jessica.

"let's close our eyes and relax." said Lorie.

They closed their eyes. When they opened their eyes, they were some place

different. "where are we?" asked Jessica. A man walked up to them. "I see you found each

other." said the man in the cape. "why are we here?" asked Jessica. "like I told each of you. You are the chosen one. You kill the vampires." said the man "why us?" asked Lorie.

"I don't know he chose you to be the chosen one." said the man. "well maybe we don't

want to be the "chosen one"" said Karen. "you will die if you don't" said the man. "like

we have much choice." said Jessica. "what about the dreams we have been having?" asked

Lorie. "well maybe they are the chosen men." said the man. "but I have been having

dreams about him being a vampire." said Jessica. "don't worry about that." said the man.

"it scares me just to even think about it." said Jessica. "tonight, at midnight come back and

I will tell you what I want you to do." said the man. And he was gone.

When they woke up the found David looking at them. "oh, David these are my

friends Lorie and Karen." said Jessica. "what is going on here Jessica?" asked David.

"nothing we were just relaxing that's all." said Jessica. "well we got to go see you at you

know what time." said Lorie. "bye Girls." said Jessica. "WHAT THE HELL IS GOING

ON HERE?" asked David. "what do you mean?" asked Jessica. "you looked like you more the just relaxing." said David "why do you say that?" asked Jessica. "who were they

anyway?" asked David. "Like I said they are friends." said Jessica. "I never saw them

before where did you meet them?" asked David. "why do you butt into what I am doing."

said Jessica. "are they friends from the hospital?" asked David. Jessica thought for a

minute. "yes, they are." said Jessica. "why haven't I heard about them." said David

"Because they are new to the hospital." said Jessica. "I never saw them there." said David.

"because they are new there." said Jessica. "I just stopped by there and you weren't

there." said David. "I took the day off today and so did they." said Jessica. "why you

never take any days off." said David. "that's because I haven't been sleeping well." said

Jessica. "I wonder why?" asked David.

Later that night around midnight Jessica left the house.

"where are we going?" asked Jessica "we can't go back to my house." said Jessica "why?"

asked Lorie "my husband will find out what we have been doing." said Jessica. "Then why

don't we go to my house my boyfriend works at night anyway." said Karen. "ok." said

Jessica.

Just then Jessica's cell phone rang.

"what do I do?" asked Jessica. "Just tell them you are working late tonight." said Lorie.

"hello?" said Jessica. "Jessie, where are you?" asked David "I am working late tonight."

said Jessica. "I thought you weren't going to work?" asked David. "well one of my ladies

friends said they would work my shift." said Jessica. "what am I going to do if Jay-Jay

has a seizure?" asked David. "He won't he has been taken his meds I made him take one

before I left for work." said Jessica. Jessica held her breath and waited for him to answer

back. "Ok I will see you when you get home." said David. "Bye David." said Jessica.

4

Jessica, Lorie, and Karen went to Karen's house.

Karen opened the door. "so, what do we do now?" asked Jessica "everybody around my

kitchen table." said Karen. They held hand's and then the man with the cape came into

view. "I see you all came." said the man "yes now why are we here?" asked Jessica. "you

all no why you are here." said the man. "no, I don't really know my husband is going to leave me and take my children from me because I am lying to him." said Jessica "then

tonight, tell him." said the man. "why?" asked Jessica "because he is the chosen man."

said the man. "he won't believe me." said Jessica. "why do you say that?" asked the man.

"Because he thinks I am working at the hospital when he doesn't know that I quit last

week." said Jessica. "why did you quit?" asked the man. "Because I have been having

these dreams and I am scared that I will mess up." said Jessica. "you won't mess up if you

don't believe you will." said the man "and how do you know this?" asked Jessica.

"because you are the chosen one all of you are and your boyfriends and husband." said the

man. "what about my children?" asked Jessica. "Have somebody watch them." said the

man. "why are we here?" asked Jessica. "let me get to it." said the man "you each get 3

stakes you get three try's each. About midnight is why the vampires will rise from them

coffins and walk among us to this day we don't who is a vampire and who is not." said the

man. "why was I having dreams about my husband being a vampire?" asked Jessica "because "they" where there when they made you dream that." said the man." why?"

asked Jessica. "how should I know?" asked the man. "well you brought us here." said

Jessica. "he is the chosen one for the men." said the man "what about mine and Karen's

boyfriend." said Lorie. "they are the chosen ones as well. One the next meeting you will

bring the chosen men with you." said the man. "like that will go well." said Jessica. "why

do you say that?" asked the man. "he won't do it." said Jessica "oh he will give him some

time." said the man and he was gone.

When Jessica came home, David was asleep on the couch. She covered him up and

went to bed herself.

The next morning, she was up fixing breakfast before he got up. "hey what smells

so good." said David Kissing her neck. "hey, let me fix breakfast." said Jessica. The twins

where up playing in their play room. "so, where were you last night?" asked David. "I

went to work." said Jessica "No I called you at work and they said you quit last week."

said David. Jessica turned pale. "where did you go Jessie." said David "I can't say." said

Jessica. "and why is that?" asked David. "because I am doing something that I don't want

to do." said Jessica. "and what is that?" asked David. "I can't say." said Jessica "well if

you are not going to tell the truth then I am leaving." said David "what why?" asked

Jessica "you are not telling the truth." said David "we are the chosen ones." said Jessica.

"what are you talking about?" asked David "come with me and maybe we can see what it

is about." said Jessica.

When the kids were off at school Jessica took David to the kitchen table.

"what are we doing?" asked David. "Close your eyes and hold my hand." said Jessica.

When he did, they were in a different world. "what is this?" asked David. The man and the

cape came into to view. "I see you are here with the chose man." said the man "who are

you?" asked David. "I am the spoken one." said the man "what?" asked David. "you kill

vampires." said the man. "what why?" asked David. "you and your wife and 4 others

people are chosen to kill vampires." said the man. "dude I have kids to look after I can't

be the "chosen one." said David "yes but you are." said the man. "you are the leader of the group." said the man. "why what for?" asked David. "because vampires are taken

over the world and we need to stop it." said the man. "why are we the ones to stop them?"

asked David. "because you are the chosen one" said the man and he left.

"why did you lie about this?" asked David. "because he told me not to say

anything." said Jessica. "you could have told me what was going on." said David "and have

you freak out" said Jessica. "yes, why should I freak out?" asked David "well don't." said

Jessica.

Later that night David and Jessica went to Karen's house.

They gathered around the kitchen Table. Karen, and her boyfriend Chris, and Lorie, and

her boyfriend James were waiting for them. "let's hold hands." said Lorie. And they did.

The man in the cape showed up. "I see we are all here." said the man. "what do you want

from us?" asked Chris. "you all are the chosen one." said the man. "chosen one for what?"

asked James. "all of you are here to kill vampires." said the man. "why us?" asked James

"because you are the chosen one." said the man "yeah yeah I know that but why us?"

asked David "you will see soon." said the man and he disappeared

5

For the next few days Jessica kept having the same dream. She would wake up

crying. David was still asleep When she got up, so she went to make some breakfast.

"there you are." said David "what I am making breakfast." said Jessica "did you have a

dream that I was a vampire?" asked David. "yes." said Jessica. "then you are right I am a

vampire." said David and his fangs came out and went into her neck. "I have been waiting

for you." said David Jessica screamed and woke up still in bed. David was not in bed with

her. She went to the bathroom. She looked at her neck and saw nothing. She went down

stairs to see where David went and found him in the kitchen making breakfast.

David went to work, and Jessica waited for the bus to pick up Jay-Jay and Grace

for school. Karen and Lorie came to her house. "we need to talk." said Lorie. "sure what

is it?" asked Jessica "did you have a dream that your husband was a vampire?" asked

Lorie. "yes, why do you ask?" asked Jessica "I think he is one." said Karen "what why do

you say that?" asked Jessica. "because the man in the cape told me." said Lorie. "he is not

a vampire." said Jessica. "yes, he is that is why he is the "chosen one" because he is one

himself." said Karen. "why do you say that?" asked Jessica. "has he been acting weird?"

asked Karen. "yes, but he is just worried about the twins." said Jessica. "have you been

having dreams about him being a vampire?" asked Lorie. "yes, but he is not a vampire."

said Jessica "you don't know that why are you having those dreams?" asked Karen. "I

don't know he said when he found he was going to leave me. Before he found out that

we were to kill vampires." said Jessica. "you should watch out and be more careful around

him more often." said Lorie. "why is that?" asked Jessica. "because he might go after

you." said Karen. "I DON'T WANT TO DO THIS WHY AM I THE CHOSEN ON?"

yelled Jessica. "because you need to kill the vampires." said the man in the cape. "is me

husband a vampire?" asked Jessica. "that is for you to find out for yourself." said the man.

"but why? Why me?" asked Jessica. "you will soon find out." said the man and he left.

When David came home, he was in a better mood than any other day.

"what is up with you?" asked Jessica. "I got a raise." said David Hugging her. "wow that

is great." said Jessica kissing him. "so, what are you going to do about us being the

"chosen one. "nothing we will have to just see it out." said Jessica. "I think we should

back out of it." said David. "we can't David we are the ones for the job I think we should

do it." said Jessica.

Later that night there was a knock-on Jessica, and David's door.

Jessica answered the door. "Lorie what are you doing here?" asked Jessica "he got me he

turned me into a vampire." said Lorie.

David was reading a book and went to see what was going on.

"what do you mean he got you?" asked Jessica. "see for yourself." said Lorie. Jessica

looked at the two holes in Lorie's neck. "Looks like a bug bite to me." said Jessica.

"how can you be so calm about this whole thing?" asked Lorie. "Because I know some of

it isn't true." said Jessica. "you can say that but you better watch what you do." said Lorie and she left. "what did she want?" asked David "nothing she thought she got bit by her

boyfriend saying, he was a vampire." said Jessica. "maybe he is." said David. "why do you

say that?" asked Jessica. "because nobody really knows who a vampire or a person that

isn't a vampire." said David. "that is what the man in the cape said. "and he is true I could

be a vampire and you would never know it." said David "are you a vampire?" asked

Jessica. "yes, but there are two types of vampires. There is a good vampire and there is the

evil vampire that only drinks blood from humans. I on the other hand drink blood from the

hospital." said David "is that why you married me because you knew you could have

blood from the hospital?" asked Jessica. "No, I fell in love with you." said David. "is that

why you got upset about me not being at the hospital anymore?" asked Jessica "yes." said

David. "well I am not going back." said Jessica. "it's alright I have other places to go."

said David. "why didn't you tell me you were a vampire?" asked Jessica. "I didn't want

you to be scared." said David. "I am mad not scared." said Jessica.

That night they went back to Karen's house. "I told her the truth." said David

Looking that them. "don't look at me that way you can't have me." said Karen. David

Laughed "I am not here to drink blood I am here to get the bad vampires off the street."

said David.

6

They gathered around Karen's kitchen table.

The man in the cape appeared. "I see you have told your wife you are a vampire." said the

man. "why are we doing this?" asked David. "as you all know there are good vampires

and bad vampires. We are here to kill the bad vampires." said the man. "and how are we

to do this?" asked Jessica. "use whatever I have given you to kill them with you have 3

months to kill them." said the man. "why us?" asked Karen. "you will all know when the

mission is done." said the man and he left.

"what do we do now?" asked Karen. They let go of each other's hands and they

were back in Karen's house. "we should go tonight David can tell where they are." said

Jessica. "why does he have to do it?" asked Chris. "Because he is one them himself." said

Jessica. "you mean he is a vampire too?" asked James. "he is a good vampire we have to

kill the bad." said Jessica. "I never heard that before." said James. "that's because you

weren't listening." said Lorie. "I was too." said James.

Later that night they went looking for vampires.

At first, they didn't see any but then one jumped out at Jessica. "are you walking alone?"

asked the man "no" said Jessica. "all I can see is you." said the man. "leave me alone."

said Jessica. "I want you to come with me." said the man. "ok" said Jessica. He took his

hand into hers. They went to a bar. "are all of them vampires?" she said to herself. "what

is your name my dear lady." said the bartender? Just a coke." said Jessica. "only a coke

you don't want to spice up your drink?" asked the bartender. "no, I am pregnant." said

Jessica. "you are? you don't look like it." said the bartender. "I just found out that I was."

said Jessica. "then why are you here." said the bartender. "I am having my husband take

me out and tell our friends." said Jessica. "I see." said the bartender. Jessica had another coke. She started to feel funny. The guy came back and saw her walking funny. "hey what

did you give her?" asked the guy "Just some rum and coke." said the bartender.

Just then David came into the bar and found Jessica trying to walk. "JESSIE

WHAT ARE YOU DOING?" asked David. "do...I... know.... you?" asked Jessica "come

on I knew this would happen." said David "hey wait she is with me." said the man. "NO

SHE IS MY WIFE." said David.

The man's fangs came out. "so that is why you came over here so you can take her

blood and make her a vampire for yourself is that it?" asked David showing his fangs.

"you're a vampire too?" asked the man "I am a good vampire." said David "let me make

you a bad one." said the man. "no, I am getting my wife and getting out of here." said

David "Not so fast you didn't pay." said the bartender. "here is some money for the drinks

now I am leaving." said David. Carrying Jessica.

When Jessica woke up, she had a big headache.

David came into the room. "I see you woke up." said David. "what happened why do I

have a headache." said Jessica "because you were drugged." said David "oh." said Jessica "don't you remember what happened?" asked David "No" said Jessica "oh man this worse

then I thought." said David "why is that?" asked Jessica. "you almost became one of

them." said David. "what how?" asked Jessica. "you went into this vampire bar and when

the bartender gave you your drink he drugged it and that is why you can't remember." said

David. "oh, I am sorry about that." said Jessica.

David went to go to work.

Are you alright?" asked David "yes I am sure." said Jessica and kissed him.

Jessica went back to sleep when she woke up the man in the cape was there staring

at her. "what? Oh, you scared me." said Jessica. "you almost failed the mission." said the

man. "I didn't know he was a vampire." said Jessica. "oh, you knew that is why you went

to the bar with him." said the man. "why are people yelling at me?" asked Jessica "because

you could have been one of them." said the man. "David saved me." said Jessica. "and

what happens if he's not their next time." said the man "he will." said Jessica. "you are

lucky to have him." said the man. "I guess I am." said Jessica and he left.

Later that day the girls met again.

"I heard about you were almost turned into a bad vampire." said Karen. "I wasn't David

saved me." said Jessica. "did you get bit?" asked Lorie "no David saved me before he

did." said Jessica. "I wish my boyfriend would do that to me." said Karen. "me too." said

Lorie.

7

Jessica, David, Karen, Chris, Lorie, and James had another meeting.

"I am not going to do this anymore." said David. "why you are a vampire yourself." said

the man. "that is different my wife shouldn't be here let me do it by myself and leave her

out of it." said David. "no, it has to be 6 people." said the man. "why?" asked David.

"because you all of you are the chosen one." said the man. "maybe we don't want to be

the "chosen. one." said Karen. "you have to do this just right all of you are the chosen

one." said the man and he was gone.

"now what are we going to do?" asked Jessica. "I have a idea?" said Karen "why

don't us girls go back into the bar and say we are looking for a date. And start to flirt with some men and when we are alone, we stab them with the stake" said Karen "what happens

if it back fires?" asked Jessica. "it won't. "said Karen.

Later that night they all got dressed and went to a bar that was filled with

vampires. "may I help you lady's?" asked the bartender. "give us all a bloody-Mary." said

Karen. "sure thing." said the man. And began to make their drinks. Some guy sitting at a

table were eyeing them. "let's go say hi." said Karen. "why?" asked Jessica "because that

is why we are here." said Karen? Karen and Lorie went to see who they were. Jessica was

sipping her drink. When I man sat down beside her. "so, it's you again why are you here

because of what happened last night?" asked the man "sorry about that. That was my

brother I guess I had to many drinks." said Jessica.

The other girls were talking to the men they picked up. And left the bar.

"are those your friends?" asked the man "yes I should go with them." said Jessica "why

don't you come to my house. It's just down the street." said the man. "sure" said Jessica.

And they left too. They walked down to a building. "I thought you lived in a apartment."

said Jessica. "this is my apartment." said the man.

They went to the building there was a coffin in the room and nothing else. Jessica's

heart was pounding. "do you want something to drink?" asked the man "no I am fine."

said Jessica. He got something what looked like wine but when he got closer to her. She

could tell it was blood. "so, what do you do for a living?" asked the man "I used to work at

the hospital." said Jessica. "what happened there?" asked the man. "I quit." said Jessica.

"so, what do you do?" asked Jessica. "I want to kiss you." said the man. "what?" asked

Jessica. He kissed her and started to take out his fangs when she started to fight back.

"NO STOP!" yelled Jessica she could get to her purse. David came running into the room.

Pushed the man off Jessica and drove the stake into his heart.

"WHAT THE HELL WERE YOU THINKING GOING BY YOURSELF WITH

HIM?" yelled David. "but we killed him." said Jessica "no I killed him not we." said

David. "why do you say that?" asked Jessica "because you could have died." said David.

The other two girls went back to Karen's house and waited for Jessica and David.

"how did it go?" asked Jessica. "you mean the two men that we went with?" asked Lorie.

"yes, so tell me did you kill them?" asked Jessica "yes." she smile. But Jessica saw her eye

teeth. She was a vampire they both were. Jessica grabbed her stake and put it right

through Lorie's heart. Karen tried to run away. "you think I am that stupid?" asked Jessica

"no but I am not a vampire he didn't get me." said Karen. "and how do I know that

Karen." said Jessica "I killed him before he got to me." said Karen. "why don't I believe

you." said Jessica "Fine don't believe me." said Karen "ok let's join together for the ones

who are left." said Jessica? David came from the kitchen with the other men. "hey where's

Lorie?" asked James "she was a vampire." said Jessica. She could see he was too. "a

vampire what do you mean?" asked James "and you are too." said Jessica and David put

a stake through his heart. "WHAT THE HELL." said Chris. "he is a bad vampire." said

David "well let's go to the kitchen table." said Karen.

They joined hands and the man in the cape came into view. "well I see there is only

4 of you now instead of six." said the man. "what does that mean?" asked David "that

means that whoever is the last 2 will be the chosen one." said the man. "so, either one of us will become a bad vampire and will be killed." said Karen "I don't like it." said Jessica.

"you will know it in your heart who the chosen one really is." said the man. "but how do

we know?" asked Jessica "you will soon know." said the man. And he was gone.

The next few days David and Jessica tried not to say nothing about the man in the

cape. Jay-Jay was sick and was taken to the hospital.

"Be careful Jessica there are vampires in the hospital too." said David she was

going to ask him how he knew that but then again, he was a vampire himself.

8

One winter night Jessica was back at work working for the hospital when David

stopped by. "we need to go to Karen's house the time has come to choose the chosen

one." said David.

When she got off work, she went to Karen's house David was already there. When

she walked into the room. She found David and Karen naked with David drinking Karen's

blood from her neck.

"WHAT THE HELL IS GOING ON." said Jessica "you are the chosen one." said

the man in the cape. "NO, I CAN'T LOSE HIM I WON'T LOSE HIM." yelled Jessica.

"you see you are the chosen one you have to kill them all to be the chosen one." said the

man. 'NO, I AM NOT HOW COULD YOU DO THIS DAVID!" yelled Jessica. "they

can't hear you. You are having a dream." said the man. "WAKE ME UP SOMEONE

WAKE ME UP." Yelled Jessica. "you are the chosen one." said the man and he was gone.

Jessica wake up. With her heart pounding. "hey, you were just having a weird

dream." said David. "oh." said Jessica she got up and started to head for the shower.

"David came into the bathroom and started to kiss her neck. "don't let me take a shower."

said Jessica.

He went to make breakfast for Jay-Jay and Grace.

David let out a yell for Jessica. She got her robe on and went to see what happened. Jay-

Jay was on the floor having a seizure. Grace was crying she picked up Grace and called

the doctor and he told them to take him to the hospital.

When they got there, they started to ask questions. "what is wrong with him?" asked Jessica. "he has gone into a coma." said the doctor. "why will he make it?"

asked Jessica. "Jessie you know how bad his seizures were." said the doctor. "yes, but I

don't work here anymore." said Jessica. "you should of know well his seizures are really

bad I don't think if we do test on him that he will make it." said the doctor. Jessica started

to cry. "hey, it's not your fault." said David.

Another hour went by and then the doctor came back.

I am sorry but the last seizure that he had just now he couldn't handle it I am sorry for

your loss." said the doctor "NO NOT MY BABY NOT HIM NO WHY HIM." cried

Jessica. "it's alright Jessie." said David. And he took her home.

Jay-Jay was laid to rest Jessica was very upset about this and couldn't get out of

bed so she couldn't see her little boy be buried. "Jessie you have to say goodbye." said

David "NO NOT TO JAY-JAY NOT TO MY BABY BOY WHY DID IT HAVE TO BE

HIM?" yelled Jessica.

"you have to face the fact that he is gone." said David. "NO, HE NOT GONE."

said Jessica she stayed in bed for nearly a week. The man in the cape to her dreams again.

"I am not the chosen one I just lost my son." said Jessica. "no but he is the chosen one and

he needs your help." said the man in the cape. " why because I am his wife?" asked Jessica

"no because you are the chosen woman and he is the chosen man." said the man. "I have

no clue what you mean." said Jessica. "you will know soon." said the man in the cape.

She didn't do anything about the Vampire thing she just stayed in bed. David was

getting worried about her. "I can't be the chosen one." said Jessica "but you are the

chosen one." said David. "but why what did I do to make the pick me?" asked Jessica. "I

just lose my son and you want me to fight a vampire." said Jessica "no you lost your son 3

months ago, you not getting out like you used to. And you gained some weight. Now tell

me why you can't fight vampires?" asked David. "maybe I don't want to." said Jessica.

"but you must you must pick up the pieces and go on with your life." said David "I can't

go on." said Jessica she took a knife and reached up to her chest. "NO JESSIE DON'T

DO IT." said David Taken the knife away from her. "WHY SHOULD I GO ON?" asked

Jessica "for me and Grace." said David "no I can't." said Jessica she ran out of the house

and got into her car. "JESSIE WAIT!" yelled David.

David called his dad and had him try to get her into his office to find out what was

wrong with her. David Followed her to where Jay-Jay was buried. "I am so sorry baby boy

I should of know you were sick." said Jessica she could hear their laughter "David came

to where she was, he found her asleep next to Jay-Jay's grave site. He had her taken to his

dad's hospital.

When Jessica woke up, she didn't know where she was. "HELP! HELP!" said

Jessica "oh you finally woke up." said David's dad "where am I?" asked Jessica "you

don't know who I am?" asked David's dad "No" said Jessica "do you know your name."

said David's dad. "no" said Jessica. "where am I?" asked Jessica "you are in a mental

hospital." said David's dad. "why what happened to me?" asked Jessica "you will find out

in time." said David's dad and walked out of the room.

9

When she woke up again, she called again, and a nurse came. "you rang?" asked

the nurse. "where am I? why am I here? do you know my name?" said Jessica "how

should I know I just work here." said the nurse "when is the doctor coming?" asked

Jessica. "he should be here around noon." said the nurse.

She came back with Jessica's breakfast. "I am not hungry "said Jessica "suit

yourself I will be back in a hour." said the nurse. And she left.

The doctor came by about 12:30 PM.

"why am I here?" asked Jessica "do you remember anything?" asked the doctor. "no" said

Jessica "you just lost someone that was close to you." said Jessica "who is it?" asked

Jessica "you will have to learn about that on your own." said the doctor. "but can't I

remember?" asked Jessica. "do you remember your name?" asked the doctor. "no." said

Jessica. "well you have a husband who is my son. Do you know his name?" asked the

doctor. "no" said Jessica she started to cry. "WHY CAN'T I REMEMBER!" yelled

Jessica "hey easy or you will have to have a shot." said the doctor. She calms down. She

was hungry so she went to see what was for lunch. "where is everybody?" asked Jessica "they are either taken a nap or reading a book. Group will be setting up in the next room."

said the lady. Everyone went to group. "now everybody says their name and why they are

here." said the nurse. When it came time for Jessica, she didn't say anything. "your name is

Jessica and you just had a family death and that is why you are here." said the Nurse. "oh"

said Jessica. When it was all over with, she went to her bedroom and went to lay down. At

dinner David stopped by. "hello Jessie, do you know who I am?" asked David Jessica

shook her head started to cry. "why are you crying?" asked David "because I have no clue

who you are." said Jessica "do you remember Grace and Jay-Jay?" asked David "I

remember something about a death in the family." said Jessica. "Jay-Jay passed away. Do

you know what from?" asked David "no." said Jessica "he has seizures." said David.

"why?" asked Jessica. "Jay-Jay and Grace have down syndrome. We adopted them when

their mother died during childbirth." said David "do you remember anything else?" asked

David. "you are a vampire." said Jessica. "not too many people know about that but yes I am a vampire." said David "he chose me and you to be the chosen one." said Jessica

"who is that?' asked David "the man with the cape." said Jessica "yes did we win?" asked

David "yes I think so." said Jessica. "I am going to give you a few more days and see how

you are then" said David and he got up and kissed her. And left the room.

Later that night she had a dream about Jay-Jay.

"mama, mama where are you mama?" said the voice. "I am right here Jay-Jay." said

Jessica "I can't see you mama where did you go?" asked Jay-Jay. "I am right here." said

Jessica.

Jessica got up and started for the door. Nobody saw where she was going. "I am

coming Jay-Jay I am coming." said Jessica. "mama mama you found me mama." said the

voice. She was walking down the side of the high way. Cars were honking their horns."

she walked in the middle of the road. "JAY-JAY WHERE ARE YOU?" asked Jessica.

She couldn't see and was thrown from the car and hit another car's windshield. They

called the cops she was dead on the scene

David got a phone call about 1:00 AM saying there was trouble at the hospital. He

He drove to the hospital.

"she got hit by a car." said his dad "is she ok?" asked David "I am sorry, but she didn't

make it" said his dad "NOOOOOOO!" yelled David. and all went black.

when he woke up, he was in a hospital bed.

"hey what is going on here?" asked David. "you pass out." said the doctor "why am I tied

down?" asked David "because we didn't want you to hurt yourself or anybody else for

that matter." said the doctor. "what do you mean hurt me?" asked David. "you were

doing a lot of things that a person wouldn't do." said the doctor. "what do you mean?"

asked David "well for one you drink blood." said the doctor. "oh" said David. "are you a

vampire?" asked the doctor. "no." said David. He lied he had to get out of here or he

would be dead. "when can I go home." said David. "right now, I just have to fill the paper

work." said the doctor.

10

When he got home, he went to bed. He drank his blood for the night.

He had a dream about Jessica. "David where are you I am looking for you where are

you?" asked Jessica. "Jessie I am here please don't go I need you I have to take care of

Grace myself." said David "I am sorry for what I have done please forgive me." said

Jessica "I won't let you go." said David. But she went away. "Jessie wait don't leave."

said David.

When he woke up his face was filled with sweat. And his heart was pounding.

When he went to go to work, he drank his morning blood. He met with Chris. "what are

you going to do about the you know what?" asked Chris. "what?" asked David "the

vampires." said Chris. "there is nothing you can do just fight them." said David.

Later that night David met Chris and Karen at Karen's house.

"we are outnumbered." said Chris. "not really if you take one at a time." said David.

"how do we do that?" asked Chris. "we can go to the vampire bar and see how many girls

we can pick up." said David. "yeah but I am not a vampire you are." said Chris. "I am not

a vampire either." said Karen. "THAT IS IT I CAN MAKE JESSIE INTO A

VAMPIRE!" said David and he Ran out the door. "bad idea dude." said Chris.

He drove to the hospital and went to where the dead people were. When he got

there he could see Jessica laying there. He opened the door. "I have come for you my

angel." said David and he bit into her neck. Then he bit into his arm and had her drink

some of his blood. Her eyes opened. "David?" said Jessica. "what happened to me." said

Jessica "you died when you got hit by a car." said David "am I a vampire?" asked Jessica.

"yes." said David. "am I good or bad?" asked Jessica "you will soon find out." said David.

Later that night Jessica, David, Chris, and Karen met at Karen's house.

"what are we going to do now?" asked Karen. "let's hold hands. When they did. They

heard voices. "get out vampire get out you don't belong with us get out vampire get out

you are not one of us." said the voice Jessica let go. "what is going on why can't I get the

man, in the cape?" asked Jessica. "I don't know." said David.

Just then the man in the cape came into view. "David what did you do?" asked the

man, in the cape. "I brought her back to life I made her a vampire." said David "yes I can see that but you should know that not a vampire are good." said the man. "yes, I know

that by now." said David "well Jessica is not a good vampire she was the chosen one now

she is the Dark Angel." said the man. "what do you mean the Dark Angel?" asked David.

"she will kill to get her way you have to kill her before she starts her killing." said the man.

"NO WAY I JUST LOST HER SHE CAN'T BE THE DARK ANGEL." said David. "yes

she is they have chosen her to be the Dark Angel." said the man. "well I will make her

change." said David. "you can't undo it." said the man. "well can't you help me?" asked

David "I wish I could, but I am only the messenger." said the man in the cape and he was

gone.

What I am going to do I can't kill her I love her. He said to himself. Jessica went

to the vampire bar. "what would you like my lady. "a Bloody-Mary." said Jessica "we

don't just use tomato juice we use blood." said the bartender. "yes, I know that is what I

want." said Jessica. "good." said the bartender. And handed her the drink.

Jessica saw a cute young guy sitting by himself. "hey how come you're not dancing?" asked Jessica. When she got there, she saw it was David. He looked depressed.

"what's wrong baby?" asked Jessica. "Nothing Jessie." said David "then dance with me."

said Jessica. "ok." said David and they started to dance. They kept dancing. "we better get

home." whispered David. "yes, that is very true." said Jessica. And they went to leave.

Later that night David had another dream.

"David, David you have to kill her why are you letting her get to you?" asked the voice. "I

can't, I can 't kill her I love her." said David "she will kill you then." said the voice. "How

can I kill her? I made her what she is." said David. "it's the only way." said the voice. "but

how can I?" asked David. "Put a stake right though her heart while she is sleeping. And a

stake showed up in his hands. He opened his eyes and saw Jessica staring at him. "what?"

asked David "you are going to try to kill me." said Jessica. "I have to Jessie they want me

to kill you because you are the Dark Angel." said David "Dark Angel?" asked Jessica

"you are evil." said David "Oh that is a bunch of horse shit." said Jessica. "the man in the

cape told me." said David. "well kill me then." said Jessica. "I am going with you." said

David. They kissed. "I love you Jessie." said David he laid her on her back and brought

the stake to his chest. And he stabbed them both.

In the morning Karen and Chris came to David and Jessica's house. When they got

there they found Grace crying. And on David's desk was a novel that Said DARK

ANGEL. "he wanted me to publish his book." said Chris. He picked up the novel and put

it into his briefcase. "where are they?" asked Karen. "it's all in the book." said Chris.

And they walked out of the house.

Made in the USA
Middletown, DE
08 December 2020